Under Firethorn

Also by Richard Stanton and published by Ginninderra Press
Enngonia Road
Seven Car Loads of What You Need

Richard Stanton

Under Firethorn

Acknowledgements

Some of these poems have been previously published:
'Situational Bogan', 'Conversion', 'St Johns' Parramatta'
and 'On Wapengo', *Quadrant*
'Stone Miles', *Milestones*, Ginninderra Press

Under Firethorn
ISBN 978 1 76109 395 1
Copyright © text Richard Stanton 2022
Cover image: Woodrow Nixon

First published 2022 by
GINNINDERRA PRESS
PO Box 3461 Port Adelaide 5015
www.ginninderrapress.com.au

Contents

Situational Bogan	9
Tom Groggin	10
Under Firethorn	12
Under Firethorn 2.0	19
War Imagined	23
Remembering	25
My Father Dying	27
St John's Parramatta	29
Conversion	30
On the Other Side	32
On Wapengo	34
Coast Watching	36
Tobias Furneaux	38
Treat Pocket	40
The End of the Beach	41
Workbench	42
Workbench 2.0	43
Black Dog	44
Door Jamb	45
Stone Miles	46
Mending History	47
Disaster Tourist	49
Daylight	51
The Walk	52
Long Walks in the 1970s	55
A Great Sadness	57
Sickbed	58
The Sundeck, 1976	59
Ancient Days	60
No Common Ground	62

In Our Town	64
Woman Posturing, 1976	66
Cues	67
Cornish Names	68
Crisp Autumn Silence	69
Your Words	71
Grand Dreams	72
Unfinished	73
Buoyant	74
Warm Rock	75
On Wimmera	76
Keeping a Watch	77
Tasting Blood	79
Enemy Within	80
The Joy of Discovery	81
Play Something	83
Passing Water	85
Griffith	86
Rollerdoor	87
Guilt	88
Homeless	89
Shane Someone	90
In Queensland	91
Tick Boxes	92
High Country Spring	93
High Country Desire	94
High Country Imagined	95
Late Spring Snow	96
Late Spring Snow 2.0	97
Drift	99
Set On Fire	100
Moments	101

Old Age	102
In the Lane	103
Kitchen Cupboard	105
Burn Me (Until I Change My Mind)	107

Situational Bogan

A book of poetry
Mountain Secrets
Launches
In Blackheath
As spring's virtue
Fills the air
With a rhododendron flourish

While at the back
Of Gardners' Inn
Mountain secrets
Of a different
Hue
Roof bolting
Coal shovelling
Are contested
By women and men
Poetic
In their own right
Over schooners of New
In the cool of the evening light

Tom Groggin

I think about Mary Lang
frequently as I drive
the Monaro where it
becomes the Snowy Mountains
a highway named twice

There off to the left
a strip of dirt named
Tom Groggin after
no person that I can find
emerging much later
if you travel east
short of Nimmitabel
where the ragged neglected railway line
crosses opposite Stanton Road

Miles of dirt meandering
through stone dark hills
vegetation-less since last
week's snowfall
mud-coloured sheep
almost indivisible against
the lee of the scree

I think about Mary Lang
riding by all those years ago
as she is now
as she imagined her
Tom Groggin

She made a fence
built a house
and like me never
turned left heading east
to sate a curiosity had she
perhaps her imagined Tom
may have been swept away
on the harsh breath of
a Monaro winter

One day I will turn into
Tom Groggin Road
drive it end to end
in memory of Mary Lang
or perhaps not. Imagining

Under Firethorn

On the bank of the river
lying looking up through branches
of green yellow
waiting almost breathless
for the sound of wings
alighting
the crack of parrots breaking
orange berries until
Pop the report of the airgun
finds its mark on
body, eye, neck
and down tumbles another
then another
because they were too stupid to
flight in fright or too
hungry to be warned off
by a well-hidden
marksboy
who learned to estimate a trajectory
over 100 yards so the dog
from two doors up
across the road on the bank sniffing the wind
felt the sting in his rump
before he heard the warning pop.

There was in early years
an overwhelming desire
a satisfying wholesome
desire to kill
and you encouraged it with
bringing home in a bright
red and yellow box
one night from work
the one thing I had been
pleading for for months
'but not yet' you both said
ganging up
not old enough to be responsible
then when unexpected home comes Diana
Model 16 made in Great Britain
almost leaping into my arms
no shooting tins off
fenceposts
no taking aim at trees
when all around flew
targets large and small
defying me to kill them
(though I did feel some sense of remorse
when the magpie fell from the clothesline
at such close range it was impossible to miss).

Why did you give me the means
provide me with
pocket money
spent weekly on cardboard
boxes of slugs hundreds
at a time with
nothing more than air
to propel them into flight?

After all, your own father
propelled a similar
hunk of lead into his
maddened head
when you were aged
the same.
Had he not had access
left behind by his own
father a member of
the local gun club
would he have found
other means?

You never ever mentioned
him or perhaps once twice
when pressed
never visited his grave
mythologised his 39 years.

Was he suicidal in the
years after discharge
medically unfit
from the army
Australia Hospital Ship
No. 1 gently named
Karoola where for more
than two years he
steamed back and forth
through Suez laden
with casualties offloaded
in Melbourne damaged
goods in Turkey, Egypt
rising to corporal then
sergeant
what got him discharged after two
and a half years
was he unprepared
on enlistment at
21 years and 11 months
for the conflict for
the mental conflict onboard
as wave upon wave
are rounded up sawn
sutured bandaged
how did he dispose of
disabled disarticulated body parts
overboard perhaps
to become Indian Ocean
fish food.

Sixteen years intervene
before you take a pea
rifle sit on a bed
jam it between your knees
or so the *Times* reported
before squeezing the
trigger did you squeeze
or pull and cause the lead to
let you linger
crying out as you did
in that cavernous two-storey sandstone
Georgian
housing so many family members
among depressed economic circumstances
heard faintly by the
sergeant of police (retired)
drinking tea in the
downstairs kitchen
we will assume
no report of his activities only
yours almost dead
prone upon the bed
the rifle between your legs
but was that
possible would not your
knees, thighs have spilled
it as they parted in
uncontrolled manliness.

Had suffered ill health and unemployment
found shot
the paper stated
self-inflicted
served his country and no doubt
suffered physical impairment thereby
silent though it was on his leaving
a daughter a son a wife
no explaining to the eleven-year-old
boy
that he must never think of him
ever
even when I asked him directly
a long time later
he diverted
did not know
he said
as we drove home past
the house
across the river to
a world where
it was lost
until the next time
he drove by.

Was it true he and his sister
and mother
had gone up country
leaving him to
his devices to
carry through his plan
(no Lifeline 24/7 then, my boy)?

How long did he plan
days hours weeks months
moments
a moment of deep
despair with a
gun at hand
on a hot summer Saturday morning?

Here in the same
long summer conditions
across the river
not far
I lie
silent breathless
under the vastness of
my pyracantha
ready to impose death
upon unsuspecting parrots.

Under Firethorn 2.0

On *Karoola*

So bright a beginning
an ornate wristlet watch
a gift from friends
before departure
at your family home
proud parents
mates
in abundance attending
a real sense of occasion
before embarkation
with the Gallipoli campaign
already two months old
enlisted to take part
in the great conflict
for the defence of
imperilled liberty
reported the local
paper

A duty
owed to your country
and the Empire
the irresistible, sacred
call of Patriotism
you would cherish the gift
you said
but what became of it
the ornate wristlet
watch

Did it keep time for you
forth and back
forth and back
steamed Karoola
did you wear it to war
or for safe keeping
deposit it with your
father

Ornate is the key
not a gift to be
taken lightly in 1915
unfit for duty in surgery wards
on board 1 AHS
I imagine
perhaps you rediscovered it
after October 10 1917
discharged as you were
from the
Australian Imperial Force
in consequence
of medical unfitness
signed off by Captain Ferguson S.O.
invalid and returned
soldiers
the ornate wristlet watch
unknown whereabouts

your own whereabouts
deemed
unfit at twenty-four when
if nåture provided
there ought to have been
so much more

At what point did you
become
unfit for duty
not immediately as
your letter home
attests
from the Mediterranean
sea
a beautiful calm day
with a warship escort
at Suez a road trip
to Cairo with
Red Cross stores
A train to Ismailia now
an hour and a half drive
but who knows then how long
and did your ship leave
Suez gathering
your party in
Ismailia
before steaming through to Port Said
and the vastness of the engagement

In Cairo you visit mosques
on Muhammadan
new year
how different
to your own
Wesleyan Methodism
as well the bazaar
where you see every
nationality
although how you
identify them is anyone's
guess

While hotels become
hospitals to
accommodate those
not killed in the Dardanelles
or other fields
more like a tourist
your enthusiasm until
in overwhelming numbers
casualties
displace any lingering sense
of real
even
the ornate wristlet watch.

War Imagined

There you are
I imagine you there
not yet the theatre
of war
you imagined

A large gun
mounted for the
remainder
of the voyage

Out from Gibraltar
into the
Bay of Biscay aka
Golf de Gascoigne
Golfo de Biscaya

Preparing to steam
to the relative
safety
of England's
southern coast

No escort warships
beyond the Mediterranean

As you I imagine
look towards
a coastline
Portuguese, Spanish,
French

Your grandfather's country
waiting north
crossing the channel
to arrive safely
two days later.

Remembering

I was going to
Dubbin your old boots
sitting there
on the shelf as they were
the day after
ANZAC day
dry and cracked
old and worn

But the Dubbin
was in the house
not here, in the shed
where the mid-morning
autumn light
landed gently.

At the back though
a very old (very old)
bottle of Joseph Liddy
Neatsfoot
lurked since 1976.

How do some things
survive so many moves
almost forgotten on
different shelves

Fished out serviceable
still, a trickle on a
Chux
absorbed almost
instantly by toecaps
mould
driven out

And your grandfather's
service medals
and your great grandfather's
service medals
gone
with some low-life
grub after
he smashes the
front door
runs off with a
safe and its contents

I had never worn them
as they were his
and his fathers

Now neither you nor I
will wear them in remembrance
of yesterday
though your old boots
are ready.
Aye, ready.

My Father Dying

On one of my father's
Dying days
He had lost interest
In everything
He revealed
To no one in particular
Though I
Was the only other
In the room

It may have been fear
Of dying
Though he displayed
No outward sign
Then or earlier

Outward signs
Were signs
Of weakness
In a man
In life or death
To remain
Unrevealed

Once or twice maybe
Fleetingly
After burying a dog or two
And he did go mildly mental
In the final months
Of his wife's life

Otherwise it might have been
Hard to discern
Where his interests lay
In his quietly contained
Eighty-one years

To lose interest
Is to lose heart
And to lose heart
Is to lose hope
Sight of any future
When the future
Holds nothing
There is nothing to hold.

In or at the end
Or both
He gave up the ghost
One of his favourite
Expressions

And I
Will never know
To what degree
He fought
Against giving it up

There were no external signs
Just the ghost
Given up with interest

St John's Parramatta

Do not linger long
looking familiarly
upward
to St John's twin spires
before which
Samuel Marsden
married
Edward and Elizabeth
soldier and convict
second fleeters both
after the
morning service
or a smiling well-meaning
Australian
of Chinese-heritage
may plead
to take pictures
of you
as a memento
of your worship
at the church
of your ancestors

Conversion

At what point does one cease to be Christian

When Sunday service attendance abates
is Easter,
is Christmas,
not enough to remain recognised

When within the boundaries
of the Christian calendar
not a thought has been had for Jesus

When children fail
to have their children baptised

When prayer
silent and secluded
ebbs

When God says so.

So hard today
to sustain momentum
as vectors from without
actively pursue a stratagem
of destruction

Not so much in earlier days
less sense of courage required
to be and be
seen to be
Christian

Your great great great grandfather
converted
somewhere along the line
from England to Wesley

Perhaps because John and Charles
demanded more
a weekly class meeting no less
additional to Sunday service

I know because
his son
prescient
more than a hundred years ago
submitted to the newly created
Mitchell custodians
his father's quarterly Wesleyan tickets
with a letter
elegantly composed and penned
beseeching, imploring
their recognition

And I
have touched them
read them
retained as they are
continuing his Christianity.

On the Other Side

Julian Casablancas writes
On the other side
On the other side
Nobody's waiting for me
On the other side

But later
He changes his mind
And sings
I know you're waiting for me
On the other side

The day my father
Died
I held his hand, watched him
Sleep
Leant over him and whispered
Wherever you go from here
Wait for me

He held my hand
His eyes stayed closed
Morphine'll do that

Okay he replied
Almost inaudibly.
Later that night
An hour into the next day
He left me.

Twenty years have passed.
I feel mean
Still
Having made such a hard
Request
Of a dying man

I want to tell him
He need wait no longer
It may be some time
Or it may be sometime soon

Deep in my soul
I want him to wait
For me still
On the other side

On Wapengo

Early crack of dawn
despite drizzle low
cloud impending rain
later mid-morning
wet anyway
launching from
ramp beside mangroves
to catch rising tide
burley up
frenzy the gars
keen to snatch
segments of nipper
pumped day before
off mudflats
on tiny fly hooks
up and in onto the ice
hardly notice as heavy rain vertical
drills into the smooth surface
like a ten-bore.

Under his oilskin
coat and hat old mate
warm and dry
feels the report
of yet another
as he
reels in gently
alert to soft
mouths and percentages
for escape
but again success
up and over the gunwhale
into the esky ice
to await the
evening when in
butter and chilli on
the grill
an extra reward
from a morning
of unalloyed joy.

Coast Watching

Before dawn under motor
you navigate through
the entrance channel
time for sail
after dawn when all-round
white
mast light is extinguished

How did you spend
your layday
Refreshing supplies
Lazing on deck
in weak winter sun
repairing
maintaining
lines, steering
other mysterious
sail powered secrets.

Like a Masonic ritual
passed down
a language of its own
from Hobart
across the body of water
named for
not the fish
the explorer

Before dawn
I watch you
through glasses
bow into two metre
swell
on your way
hundreds of miles
warmth of
the north Queensland winter
siren calling

So long ago
Cutters ran and ran
against
the same routes
Cutters
only imagined now

As limited coast stations
keep watch on you
embodying
those traders as
you slip past
the rockwall
before dawn

Tobias Furneaux

One thousand vertical metres
below Nimmitabel
on the coast
thousands of blue fin are being
packed in ice
while the ice around Nimmitabel
remains on the lee
side of the road
from last night's
snowfall

You imagine you are
in Scotland in your
Harris tweed your
fingerless mitts
black felt Stetson
new Meindl walkers
rucksack packed
with everything to set
out across the gorse
as the Nimmitabel
four degree afternoon
gives way to the
warmer coastal winter
seascape

You are though not in Scotland
but in the National Library
reading about
Tobias Furneaux
deciding if he is deserving
of your biographical
attention
for the foreseeable future
or if there will be
a foreseeable future
as once more you
drive passed Nimmitabel's
Tom Groggin Road
without turning in to it
to see where it goes
after so many years

As the great navigator
lies entombed in
Stoke Damerel parish church
waiting for your decision.

Treat Pocket

Come back almost
every time
200, 100, 50 yards
out
up goes the arm
up go the ears
come back you do
even when
on rare occasions
nothing is there
to find
it was a trick
a good one
how far would you
run
on the scent
on the beach
on the track
after rangas
after noon
before dusk
before dinner
before they settle
for the night
waiting
until you appear
to come back
every time
for treats
from the pocket.

The End of the Beach

The end of the beach looks far
to walk most days
seems longer as days grow
shorter
not today though as sun rises
over still sea
the end looks not like an end
at all
a beginning to be walked
and walked again
and again
the only company the dog
and a clear wind
ready for anything

Workbench

Dry as a chip the old
workbench in the shed
for 20 years
more
You had it twenty
probably more like 60
made way now
last rites
up the chimney
burned bloody hot
enough to keep you
warm as toast
four nights in a row
good solid redwood
it was
hot as buggery
it burned

Workbench 2.0

Burning the bench again
tonight
a leg this time
too long to fit in the
grate
straddling across the top
as fingers of flame
rush upward
cracking against
years of embedded oil
old chemicals

Bolts too difficult
to remove
even with new blades in the
reciprocator
so they can lie
gently
in the flames and embers
until tomorrow
when curled slightly
they cool enough
to be swept up
in the ashes like
a handful of
Gram Parsons lyrics.

Black Dog

You ought to sugar soap
the kitchen door
scrape back old paint
to near timber
in preparation
for the new

When (or if)
the black dog
lopes off

Door Jamb

The door jamb
jams
despite shaving
planing with tools
that fail
to do their jobs

At wits end
in the shed
a rebate plane
A rabbet to
the hearing impaired
(also see gunwhale
where is Alex Buzo
when you need him)

The old rebate
handed down
unused in forty years
iron still sharp
peels
slivers

Shaving with the grain
until success
screen door slams
jamb free
thanks to
a grandfatherly rebate

Stone Miles

There were stones beside the highway, carved, setting forth
new distances in Imperial measure from a starting point
a metaphor to begin then tangible it too emerging from stone
the Obelisk, standing, in bold recognition of its Governor.

Sandstones carved and embedded beside the Great Western
enumerated in Roman all the way to who knows where now
certainly not Bathurst, nor Mt Victoria, not even Penrith
where once thirty-five stood as rough ashlars counting down.

The Great Road between Civilisation and a bold Frontier.
Give Mr Cox the task they said and the Governor in his infinite
wisdom did with the same sense of occasion anoint Mr Cureton
carver of milestones, and obelisks, and dwarf stone walls.

I remember as a small child seeing them from the back seat
of the grey Morris Minor in barren landscape till neon from
Broadway breweries lit my imagination beyond apprehension
all thoughts of straight great roads falling backward forever.

Now the milestones are gone, the Imperial is a faded memory.
To travel the great Mr Cox's road from Mr Cureton's Obelisk
through Parramatta and on to Penrith requires nothing more
than to listen to satellite navigators with Chinese accents.

Mending History

While communities mend
Following
Ravening fire
Fences also are keen
To mend
Government largesse
Some say too late
Pitches human resources
Into towns
And villages 'decimated'
Opine media peeps
But more than one tenth
Has been cut from
The heart of them
As too
History needs mending
In the aftermath
Of the media
Firestorm

Courageous, childlike
In borrowed uniforms
They stand without irony
Before cameras
Fanning flames of
Outraged imagination
With their inaccuracies

History as much as bushland
Becomes the victim.

What will it take
To recalibrate
Realign the damage
If it is not too late
Tipping
Us into an abyss
Fabricated
Beyond historical recall.

Disaster Tourist

'They' closed the Monaro Highway
Whomever it was had the power
Delegated to them probably the same
As 'they' who remain blameless
For burning national parks, state forests
Caused by nothing less than climate change 'they' say

Again today forty-three degrees
Too much for some as the
Orroral Valley blazes away
Braced by a Beaufort nine nor'easter
So a drive to Namadgi to see what's afoot
Is now out of the question

Joe Murphy was the ultimate disaster tourist
Used to take pix for the *Manly Daily*
All year then go off
To Africa or Middle East hot zones
On his three weeks' holiday
Photograph war, destruction, other stuff

So not down to the high country today
No drive to the mountains or the coast
If 'they' decide to close the King's
Which 'they' could at the drop of a hat
Do 'they' still know that expression

Maybe a couple of hours
In the museum air-conditioned
Gawk at Matisse
Picasso
A twenty-eight-dollar entry fee
Might as well be a closed highway
A brake on the enthusiasm

So off to the room on the left and into the
'Australian' collection to view free
Arthur Streeton *Golden Summer* (my favourite) 1889
Charles Condor *Hot Wind* 1889
Streeton (again) *The Spirit of the Drought* 1896
Here they hang now
Quietly

No longer privileged as 'they' who have the power to
Recast the story of nineteenth century Australian art
Charles and Arthur now imagined as non-indigenous
Where past present and future 'they' say exist as one

Masterpieces of Australian impressionism
Recast as pictures by non-indigenous artists.
Disaster for tourists whichever way you carve it.

Daylight

So pleasant at this
Moment
Dawn
The last
Before the
Rush to catch
The hour
As six months
Uninterrupted
Is saved
For
Some forgotten purpose

The Walk

Dust off your maps
your boots
find your compass,
if you can.

Register your plb
how many
where
how long
plan your food
five days of dehyde
not good
for ageing bodies.

New rucksack excites
old memories
rambling
below the surface
beneath the ordinary senses
of bigger adventures
of which you
are
reminded
is the past tense
of disaster.

So you plan
and plan again
allow for
fires
dry in the Alps
beyond almost
recall.
1970s. Perhaps.

Dried to a crisp
same as now
fewer huts
on route
policies of national
parks
unfathomable
mystifying
as dry layer
upon layer upon
layer upon
layer
beds underfoot
cracks
sparking not surprisingly
spontaneously.

But by the time
you're ready to
start
it will all be over
blackened, scorched
earth
smells lingering,
smoke in leafless
branches
but all of that
is imagined.

The track waits untouched
yet dry
it may soon ignite
so we must pass
quickly my son
if we are to inhale
the bliss of the bush.

Long Walks in the 1970s

Overland
        Route Burn
                Green Stone
                      Hooker
                              Brassies

Kerries
        Frenchman's
                Victoria Falls
                      Bluegum
                              Red Rocks

Wolgan
    Brindies

Solo days on end
Endless
No risk assessment
Hazard reduction plans
Get there
Hitch
        Train
                Bike
No contact
Home when you
Walk in the front door.

Forty years and age
Require
Risk management
Technology
Hurdles erected
Mainly by
Anxiety-overloaded
Well-meaners.

Two score later years and ten
Contemplating Kiandra
Taking five days to Tharwa
A tally of hazards
From recent shorter
Adventures
(Past tense of disaster)

Hocus Pocus (rotator cuff)
    Breakfast Creek (smashed elbow)
        Cox's River (dehydration)
            Mt Bogong (exhaustion)
Rodriguez Pass (exhaustion)
    Perisher (thumb sprain)
        Farm Creek (snow hole fall)
What could possibly go wrong
Now six months have gone since last adventure

Do not let them stop you
With their talk
Rage
Rage against the dying of the walk.

A Great Sadness

I am struggling
Mentally and physically
With the
Lockdown
Not because I
Am disabled
By government proscription
Nor because I am unwell
I am not.

My struggle
Is to overcome fear
Induced by statistics
Horrifying pronouncements
And despair.

Fear has disabled me.
Fear that
If I survive
Nothing will change.

Sickbed

From your sickbed
Self-isolating
You imagine
Salmon fishing on the Spey
Mary Lang
Writing
Sitting comfortably
In Gunderoo
With
Tom Groggin.

You try to recall
William Cowper's
Let There Be Light
But falter
After
God moves in mysterious ways.

Imagine
Two drowned Narooma fishermen
A few moments
Painless
Until soon after
All concentration
Plays out in the present.

The Sundeck, 1976

Mike Williams
lent you his guitar
to play during the break

Trevor Knight
critiqued your
microphone technique

John Ewbank
asked if you
mountaineered
or just liked wearing big boots

Ruth Ward
wore a patch over her
right breast
that read
Hell on Wheels.

Ancient Days

Ancient days
Ancient days
Memories flood
Back
Ancient days

As bushfire smoke
Triggers
Ancient days

Smoke filtered sun
Imagining
Old ways

Then
Off you went
Off you went
Joined a sect

Not John Wesley
On that I
Checked

Never saw you
Again
Down the years

Forty in all
Since you left
Strewn tears

Ancient days
Ancient days

When axis mundi
Tilts
Spring into autumn

No Common Ground

Battles go on in this strange little town
For the fishos and hipsters there's no common ground

There's work for a tradie if you don't mind a drink
But fill in your paperwork or you're likely to sink

'A two-million build' says the bloke in the club
for eighteen months, that'll keep us in grub

He's spruiking up a new house on the beach
where the Sydney incomers can stay out of reach

Now the renters have gone 'cause the place is so hot
While corona stops travel, hipsters buy up the lot

Old fishos sit quietly sipping ale at the club
As the wealthy (from Bondi) buy and reno the pub

A two-bedroom fibro that once went for a song
now sells for a million geez, something's gone wrong

The battles are fewer as days become years
Church congregations through masks and their tears

Pray for some permanence before it's too late
With the faithful reduction grows a secular state

When you get old you just have to go
No aged care here, no end to the flow

A market is built on the nursing home site
brings in the tourists doesn't give 'em a fright

When they head for the beach with coffee in hand
From two-score takeaways depending on brand

Chock-a-block with gelato and overpriced bread
You won't find a doctor unless you're near dead

But it's rained so hard recently actually, quite a lot
that the digger can't dig fresh new cemetery plots

Travel down from the parlour but stay in the hearse
While mourners can't sing nor recite you a verse

More battles go on in this weird little place
where bridges with one lane are saved by her grace

While old folk who've lived here all of their years
are sent off uncared-for unremembered unfeared

Council builds bike paths to cater it must
for the hipsters with carbon the hippies can rust

In come the tourists with money to burn
pushing in front because it's their turn

In come the big boats that are too large to fail
out to the canyons where the albacore sail

Out to a thousand fathoms they speed
hunting the blue fin, far more than they need

Then back to the pub for an over priced meal
rubbing shoulders with hipsters good for a deal

Battles go on in this strange little town
Where there will likely be never, no common ground.

In Our Town

Four or five generations
living in one town
close by
related directly
by blood
marriage
children of
boys & girls
interwoven
by nothing more than
hot bedding
any time it gets too tough

Courage said John Wayne
is being scared to death
but saddling up anyway.
seems some of this
town's cowboys
take him literally

Four generations
living in one city
far apart
may see each other
when there is need
for a sense of occasion

Until the occasions
become less frequent
or the catalyst
ceases to be

Four generations
can live in the city
with excuses
for the widening drift
of time
meeting at funerals
for reasons
yet to be abolished

Woman Posturing, 1976

'Oh look,' said the woman
in hippy clothes and hair
'They have oranges'
as she hesitated in the road
looking upward through the gate
to the grove
where trees laden

'They wont mind'
'It's for the little girl'
she said
believing her words
herself as she stumbled
in the dirt up the
embankment tugging
tugging plunging armloads
until her Indian print skirt
almost tore
under the weight and
you could see her
bony hips protruding above
the sag

Cues

We take our cues
From parental views
In those first formative years

Old Mr Penellum
In his blue singlet
Leaning over his front gate
In mid winter afternoons

Not in so many words
To be avoided
Respond politely
To his jibes about
Football being as important
As piano

Me now in mine
Preparing beds for lime
As Chinese scurry by in fear

Cornish Names

You didn't know
Penellum was a
Good Cornish name

Childhood bigotry
Made it more sinister
Like a wog or a spick
Or worse a dirty gypo

Others to be shunned
Cornish mainly
Trevaskis
Trewhela
Tremayne
Settled in their homesteads

But no difference there
They too had arrived
To settle
At Bird's Eye Corner
Until the river
Rose (unlike any foreknown pol)
Too many bleddy times

Still, low-lying on this side
But not so frequent
The flooding.

Crisp Autumn Silence

Crisp autumn
silence at sunrise
punctured by first,
second,
third gear
not automatic
but takes you back
a moment later
to a time
when
eagerness to correctly identify
each individual
base note
from miles away in the silence
One-seven-nine
One-eight-six
twin Holleys
bored out thirty
mill
vee eight
Gee Tee Ess
stainless extractors
pride in recognition

No longer relevant
except for
the occasional glimpse
of Aitch Ess Vee
Oh Tee Argh cold filter
among two litre
turbo squeakers
high-pitched to match
modernity

But not today
in the quiet of breaking dawn
there goes
deep throated
Gee Tee Ess three-two-seven
with a base note
deeper than the crisp autumn
to pitch you right back
into nineteen sixty-eight.

Your Words

You watch
As words
Like spring buds
Blossom

You wait
As words
Like autumn leaves
Fall

To be swept together
Into emotive
Coherence

Grand Dreams

Surrounded by Chinese
And a smattering of other
Asians
Koreans, for example
Your grand dreams
Vanished
Years before
Each one knocked down
By fear
Or financial constraints
Fear belonging to others
Financial shared
Priorities poorly
Prioritised

Grand dreams
Owning a country newspaper
A small acreage
Beyond your station
Say some with no ambition
Beyond living in peace
With these Chinese
Invaders.

Unfinished

Sat out amongst
unfinished
as a cold autumn wind
pulled at angophora branches
twisted at curmudgeonly angles

Think dispassionately
as you do
of lost loves
down the years
in multiples of ten
plus the lustrum
if needed

Forage backwards
as far as you like
or care to remember

Buoyant

It's better
you
with your nothingness
drag me down
to share
your despair
than
for you
to ever attempt
buoyancy
on my terms.

So here I am
What now?

Warm Rock

You can't go back
they don't remember you
you can't go forward
they don't care who you were

Sitting against warm rock
again
watching climbers
in the noonday sun

Are you
still in the world after
so many years

On Wimmera

Axis Mundi
on the Wimmera
in April
on its axis
with purposiveness
the diurnal

You felt the turn of the earth
out on the Wimmera Plain

Keeping a Watch

To define
to provide definition
to a life
disarmed, fragmented
a new timepiece
paid for
with insurance money
due
since break-in

Loss of old watch
which defined
proscribed
thirty-eight years
not so long
will the new one
have
to define
as the end
is closer than that
not yet
in sight
but closer

But it was not the watch
that defined
it was the idea of the
watch
imagined as the
definition
signifier

rather than sign
rather than signal
though the event
itself
was truly signal

Tasting Blood

You tasted blood
when you were three
after you had fallen
from a tree
across your face
it flowed free

Or perhaps it was a fence
it makes no difference
but it was you
and if you close your eyes
you can guarantee
the taste, the smell
returns as if it
happened yesterday

Enemy Within

Where are they from
These enemies who want us gone
Not Cornwall
Not England
Not Scotland
They hear no pipes in the glen
Imagine no corries, no bhen
St Pirran with his white cross
on a black ground
by stealth they come
we hear no familiar sound

The siege this time
is insidious
no ships pounding shorelines
no troops singing from the pines
there will be no call to arms

The Joy of Discovery

Now you have it
evangelise
facebooking proselytise
leave no ground
untilled in your quest
for knowledge
reject reject reject
all that you knew
for the new

Never again
acknowledge nor even
speak of
western civilisation
from whence you came
embarrassing in its
greatness

evangelise
proselytise
the magical world of
on country
smoking ceremonies
like Disney
evangelise
proselytise
beat your twittering
facebooking followers
to within an inch of tolerance

woke-fill the heads of your kiddies
so they may forage
for their existence
on bended knee
dream dreams of serpents and rainbows
within the joy of discovery

Play Something

When she said
play something wistful
and melancholy
you had no idea what she meant.

Puzzled she must have
read your country boy
ignorance
native instincts
you were told
but they were of no use here.

Above 10,000 feet
in a warm dry hut
hanging on to a borrowed
guitar
so she adds
Leonard Cohen, Suzanne
which was not within
your
repertoire of
Neil Young
John Denver
good old country
pickin'.

She faded into
the background
along with her stupid
lefty middle class
university-educated
requests.

But deep down you
hated her not her but the
not knowing
there was no key
for you to unlock
those doors behind which lurked
everything you wanted
to learn.

Passing Water

Does it hurt
when you pass water
asked the medico
in an attempt to
discern a urinary tract
infection

You remained
unsure how to answer
as you lived
by a river which
you
passed every day

Griffith

What would you possibly do in Griffith
for three nights
replied the dopey old codger
at the next table
at the café
at Hunters Hill
to a statement from his senile lunch partner

Perhaps the question
rhetorical as it may have been
might be better put as
what would you possibly do in Hunters Hill
after eating at the café
after drinking coffee
dozing in your chair

Rollerdoor

Carry an empty beer keg
down your leg
or at least it looks
like it's strapped on
as you, slanted way left,
hobble it towards the
pick up place

from the roller door
on the side of the club
all the way to the driveway
would it not have been
easier given its emptiness
to kick it on its side
roll it from roller door

wouldn't have looked
nearly as good but
as it did splinted to your leg
a two legged barrel ramble
when the roller door goes up

Guilt

You had a choice
But did not know
Which was the safe path
Which way to go

With your head,
With your heart
One filled with logic
The other, not too smart

You grind you teeth
Your aching head
In exchange for a
Day of love in bed

Guilt throws up
A monstrous wall
Too large to knock down
Or from which to fall

You had a choice
And made it so
Your choice was right
As only God will know

Homeless

You say in your most disarming voice
for two years
homelessness has been your choice

Now here's a paid-up bond on a room
so anxious
flight your response: kaboom

Shane Someone

And then you can no longer remember
their names
as if they never existed
fragments somewhere at the end
a click in time
a face faceless
nameless
Shane someone
wrote about Sydney's dying pub
music
at the hour of its death
a drummer
that much remembered
Shane someone
with a PhD about pub music
Shane someone
but within moments
the memory and the triggering
of it by either the whisky
or the dog
or the cool of the evening
or the
will be gone as quick as it came
Shane someone
now no longer relevant
nor enough to become
concerned that memory
of the moment is no longer

In Queensland

There you were in Queensland
in your caravan
in the warm winter sun
three score years
and ten plus four
then, no more

Now a year on
your house on the coast
far south
sold sight unseen to someone else
unknown in town
doing a bit of a demo
then a full reno
seems to be a thing
in these as some might say
uncertain times

One thing is certain though.
You won't be coming back.

Tick Boxes

We tick boxes
Twice
Once going up
Twice going down
Going up
Ticks
Signify exploits
Sign-off achievements
Going down
Signal limitations
Limits
Of a life well lived

High Country Spring

You sit among snow gums
on a long-dead trunk
still hard
and feel neither
angry nor old
as the sun
burns off the last
of the season's snow

And even a fall
on ice
as spring grass
grabs at your skis
and you plummet
to the deck
angry old age
is not with you
today
in
high country spring

High Country Desire

High country
desire
is it one more
tick in the
box
with the door closing
on past times

Is it enough
to want to
come back
to
frame dead snow gums

Or
is memory enough
do you need
to
remember dead snow gums

High Country Imagined

Frame yourself
Against the image

Of
Dead snow gums

Late Spring Snow

When you fall in a
hole in the snow
where in summer
a creek runs
and your left leg
bends back behind
your head

Howl
then try hard to extricate
yourself
and your rucksack

Praise
not this time
God
but the Aldi
exercise bike
and your 10-kilometre mornings

Late Spring Snow 2.0

When you look
up
at the afternoon sun
slanting
across
late spring snow
your head
in
you can do it mode
tomorrow
skin up
ski down
skin up ski down
clarity
of purpose

But head
forgets
attachment to body
that so far
refuses
to
run
jump
anything
except walk
early
and then only
to the next suburb
and back

As the sun
looks back
as the snow
as the mountain
look back
at you
challenging
angry oldness
in which
another
mile or two
of youth
sloughs

Drift

Who throws out
the challenge

I do arcs
the sun
no I
drifts the snow
'tis I
cuts in the
day
who has most to offer
as limits meet limitations

Have you
earned
that
cigar and single malt

Set On Fire

Out there
may be
challenges
in here the food
must be prepared
fire must be set
defib must be checked
operational
wood must be chopped
wood
must
be
chopped

Moments

No longer
listless
each tick
in
each box
as the list
falls backward
through
a life
collecting
each and every
moment of being
until
none remains

Old Age

What remains
to be done
is dependent
variables
control the outcome

What remains
to be seen
is a function
of remaining

In the Lane

In the lane the amiable woman
plucks weeds
the dahlias you remark
after she offers first greeting
are a delight to behold
enough for her to
smile
to thank you as she
beams proudly and
rightly as you see
further behind the palings
banks of roses two three four
bordering an immensity
of vegetables
themselves in orderly rows
in early afternoon sun.

To pause is to have her
provide a story there is time for
to exchange names
she will lift some dahlia bulbs
I can let you have
some she says
next winter when I separate them
You will call back then
but not before
admiring the chilli bush
ripe plump among
the butternuts beans and beets.

Come in then you shall have some
one will be enough
five six are cut before you can protest
tumbled into your palm
deep red
bright green stems
in contrast where the dear lady
has sheered with deft
sharpness of secateurs.

You part company
as the chillies sit
snugly in a pocket along with house keys
you continue along the lane
contemplating the probability
of returning
in winter
contemplating the possibility
of rice with chillies
for dinner.

Kitchen Cupboard

The mountain takes a toll
When you neglect to set a goal
Seeking and destroying
Every soul

The kitchen cupboard's bare
Cracked lino starts to wear
So back out to the highway
In sun and dust and glare

Wings span out the space
And drift between each face
One sallow, one bereft
And one of grace

Take each in their own part
Somewhere back towards the start
Remember in their eyes
You shot an arrow in the heart

When fingers play a tune
You stand to leave the room
But don't echo cries of doom
In my direction

And you, you talk of meaning
In the fast lane of your dreaming
Drinking single malt and screaming
Of imperfection

The kitchen reeks of white
And floods out all the night
Until your finger flicks a light
In her eyes.

Burn Me (Until I Change My Mind)

Burn me scatter me
across the High Plain
when the wind gets up to
forty knots
and the cattle once
again graze on lush grass

My will
always chosen
burial
but where
when there is no home

Some in Cornwall
some Penrith
the Plains of Emu
so the High Plain of Bogong
for me
ash in the wind
by the side of the road
with its yellow
above-the-snowline
markings.

www.ingramcontent.com/pod-product-compliance
Lightning Source LLC
Chambersburg PA
CBHW071126130526
44590CB00056B/2452